Not an Oxymoron:

Standards-Based Fun in the Classroom!

30 Projects and Activities for Middle School Language Arts

Garrett M. Carter

Printed by CreateSpace

Background story

Truth be told, I never set out to create a book. However, during my first two years of teaching, I developed a variety of standards-based projects and activities that created a renewed sense of excitement for learning amongst my students. In fact, my students often told me that they didn't mind completing my projects because they were fun; quite an accomplishment to hear that from adolescents! One day, during my planning period, I approached a co-worker with an activity that I created. She responded by saying that it was something she would pay for. At that moment, I realized that we as teachers are all authors. We constantly walk our students through the entire writing process, so why not go there ourselves? I took that teacher's comment and...now I'm an author! *Thanks, N.M.!*

How to use this book

The user-friendly table of contents lists the projects/activities, page numbers, and related standards. The introductory pages contain a brief description of all projects and activities. With a different intent, or slight modification, you may find that additional standards apply. At the time of this publication, over forty states have adopted the English Language Arts Standards (as determined by the Common Core State Standards Initiative). However, to ensure that you get the most out of each project and activity, cross reference the materials from this book with the standards for your state.

Why this book?

- Standards-based
- Promotes collaboration
- Engaging
- Fun
- Relevant

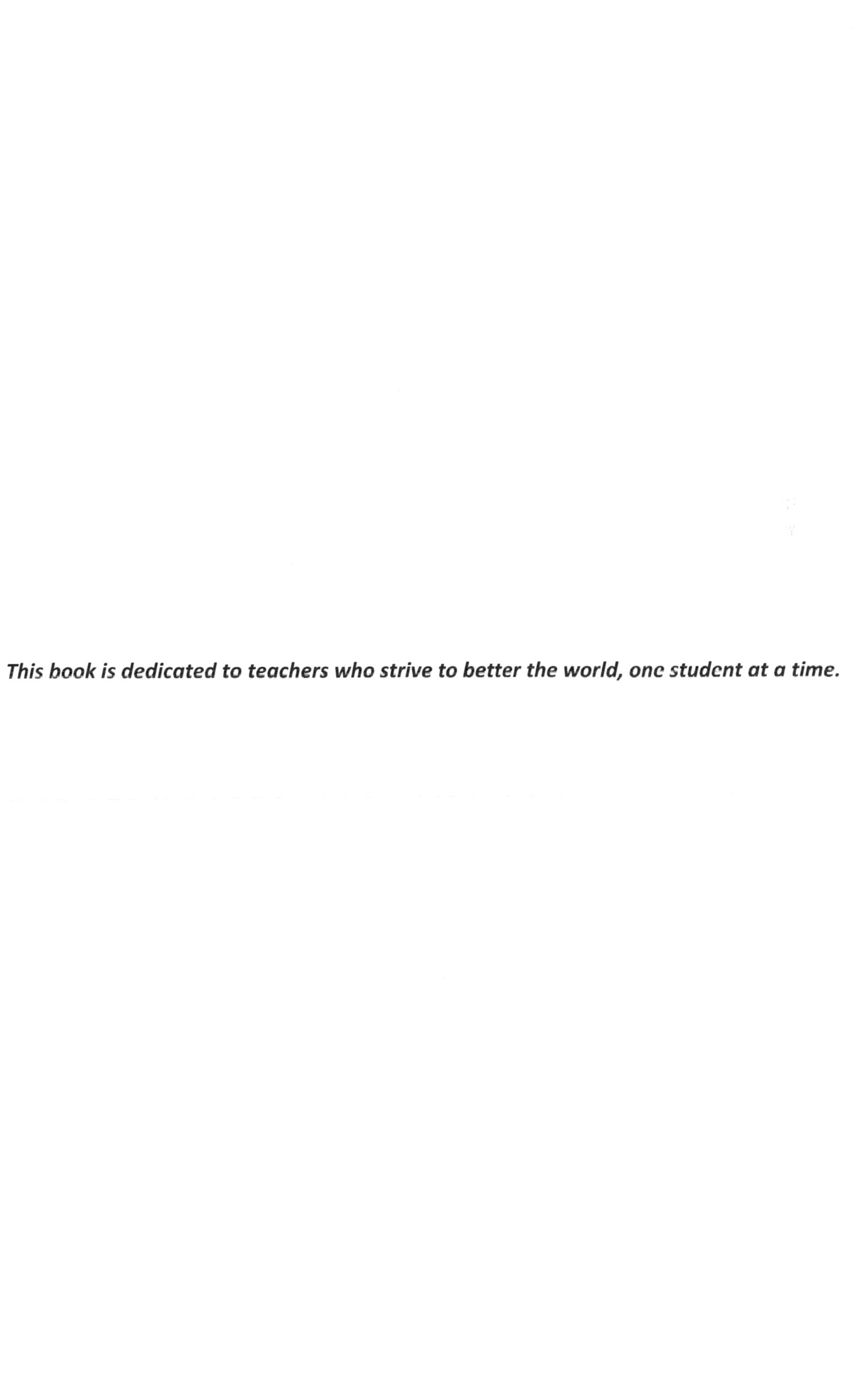

This book is dedicated to teachers who strive to better the world, one student at a time.

Table of Contents & Alignment of Standards*

*All of the projects and activities included in this book are standards-based and/or support skill development of the English Language Arts Standards (as determined by the Common Core State Standards Initiative). To ensure these projects and activities support your curriculum, refer to the English Language Arts Standards for grade-specific information. This book has not been evaluated, reviewed, or endorsed by the Common Core State Standards Initiative.

Project and Activity Introductions

Disney Movie Project (pgs. 7-10)

Aaaahhh! The start of a new school year! All of these new and smiling faces! Now what?

Have you found yourself excited about the start of the school year, but unsettled by the fact that you are unsure of what your students know? If so, you are not alone. After pre-testing my 7th graders, it became clear to me that my students were all over the place when it came to their understanding of literary terms.

I knew I needed a project that would grab their attention, but teach them at the same time. So, what to do? What else? I turned to Mickey Mouse and his friends and created the Disney Movie Project. Surely, all of my 7th graders would identify with a good Disney movie.

I decided my class would watch 45 minutes of Disney's *The Princess and the Frog*. After watching a portion of the film in class, I introduced the Disney Movie Project and we completed part of the project together. Not only did this clear up any potential problems with comprehension of the project itself, this also served as a way for students to learn, identify, and interact with literary terms. The Disney Movie Project provides real-world application in a fun, innovative, and engaging way.

Start popping that popcorn!

Use that Form: Narrative, Biography, and Poetry & Use that Form: Fact, Fiction, and Fantasy (pgs. 11-14)

"For your next project, you are going to create biographies which I'm sure you've all done before, right? RIGHT?"

While students may read many genres, they are often unable to explain the differences between them. These activities engage students and expose them to several genres.

Get that writing hand ready...

Flip & Roll (pg. 15)

Do your students know literary terms, but rarely use them in their writings?

In language arts classrooms, it is fairly common to point out examples of literary terms while reading novels. Students can identify literary terms, but it is a completely different story when it comes to incorporating examples of these terms into their writing. With this activity, students use literary terms in their writing, determined by how the die lands.

Roll out those literary terms!

Coloring Conflict 1 & **Coloring Conflict 2 (pgs. 16-17)**

Character versus...versus...versus...I don't know!

Students can often identify conflict, but sometimes struggle with determining the different types of conflict. With this activity, students encounter several conflicts and color the boxes according to the type of conflict presented. After completing this activity, students receive additional practice by creating their own conflicts, trading papers with another student, and coloring the conflicts created by that student.

Sharpen those colored pencils!

Flip It (Fact and Opinion, Simile and Metaphor, Alliteration and Onomatopoeia) (pgs. 18-20)

"Take out a sheet of paper. Number one through ten. Write five sentences with facts and five with opinions." BORING!

With the Flip It activities, students essentially complete the above, but with a...flip. Instead of dictating to students how many of each term they will practice, you are leaving it up to a coin to decide. Students will be so excited that they get to flip coins, it won't matter that they're completing school work!

Grab the hammer...it's time to crack open Mr. Piggy Bank!

Name that Symbol (pg. 21)

Students read five short stories and then draw a symbol that represents what each story is about. After they are finished, they write their own short stories and a partner creates symbols to match. This works great as an in-class activity, or students can complete their individual part as homework and the partner work in class the following day.

This assignment may symbolize the future success of your students!

Totem Pole Symbolism (pg. 22)

Students apply their knowledge of characters from a text and show their creativity. With this activity, students fill in totem poles with symbols that represent characters. Students also complete a totem pole that represents their own personality. You'll be so impressed with their creativity that you will want to post these all over the room.

Get out the tape!

Project and Activity Introductions

Food for Thought (pg. 23)

Who doesn't love food?

Students compare characters in the text with different food items. As an extension activity, students may bring the food to class.

Sounds tasty!

Pass the Plot (pg. 24)

Students work in groups of six to practice the plot diagram. If students get stuck, they have their group members to assist them. This activity helps students understand how each part of the plot plays a role in the development of a good story.

Pass out those index cards...

Plot Plate (pg. 25)

Students use paper plates to plot a story. This activity works great as a final book project and makes a great decoration.

"Stop drooling...this plate is not for eating!"

Plot that Show (pg. 26)

Similar to the Disney Movie Project, this activity is less comprehensive and focuses exclusively on plot. Depending on the age and grade level of your students, you may need to specify what shows or networks you consider appropriate.

Did I mention how cool you will be because your students get to watch TV in order to complete their homework?

Prewriting Worksheet (pg. 27)

"But I don't know what to write about..."

If you teach language arts, you have undoubtedly heard this phrase. This prewriting worksheet can be used as a tool to help students get started with writing assignments. The teacher chooses possible settings and students roll dice to determine which one will be used. Students briefly describe characters and highlight major plot points on the plot diagram. Students also incorporate several literary elements into their writings.

Magazine Writing Activity (pg. 28)

This writing activity causes students to think outside of the box. To begin, only pass out the top portion of the directions to students. Once students have finished cutting out pictures from their magazines, pass out the rest of the instructions. This activity forces your students to stretch their imagination and create an interesting story!

Let the fun begin!

Infer It (pgs. 29-30)

"That's correct, but how did you know?"

Students are often able to determine what is being inferred, but have difficulty in pointing out the evidence that guided them to their conclusion. With this activity, students read various scenarios, identify what is being inferred, and explain the specific textual evidence for their conclusion. Students then create scenarios of their own that contain inferences, trade papers with a partner, and...

I'm sure you can infer the rest...

Enhance Your Vocabulary (pg. 31)

"'A lot'...is there a better word you can use instead?"

This activity helps students build their vocabulary by selecting more effective words. Students may complete individually or work in small groups.

"Excellent! 'A lot' can often be replaced with many, several, and multiple!"

Nutrition Facts and Ingredients & **Coupons (pgs. 32-33)**

Students compare and contrast information, answer several questions, and use their analytical skills to decide the healthier product or better deal.

Get out the scissors…time to do some clipping!

C U Online & **Hit the Cell (pgs. 34-35)**

Today's kids spend several hours a day on computers and cell phones. Both of these worksheets grab students' attention by embracing technology. Students create dialogue between characters for online and cell phone conversations.

N-joy, ttyl!

Talk to Me: an Interactive Reading Tool (pg. 36)

This graphic organizer ensures that students think critically as they read. Students write summaries, make predictions, identify critical details, and create questions to ask characters and/or the author. This tool may be used as a reading homework assignment, a pop quiz, or to aid a read aloud.

Students will interact with books in an entirely new way!

Create a Soundtrack (pg. 37)

Students imagine the novel they are reading is being turned into a movie and they are in charge of adding music to five scenes. They compare the text of the novel to the text of song lyrics to identify appropriate songs. Students also design a CD cover. As an extension activity, they may actually create a soundtrack.

This assignment will be music to your students' ears!

Bime line (a book time line) (pg. 38)

A bime line?

A bime line is a book time line ("bime" comes from merging the words **b**ook and t**ime**). For this activity, students work with specific pages from their book to create a time line of the book's events. Make sure they understand that the boxes must be completed in chronological order.

Book Brochure (pg. 39)

Students select three chapters from their novel and create summaries, identify symbols and literary terms, define words, ask questions, and make connections to the text.

With this project, students will definitely make a connection!

Editor-in-Chief (pg. 40)

Students create a magazine based on an assigned or chosen topic. They design a front cover and write three articles that appear in the magazine. A great end-of-novel project!

Your students may now add "Editor-in-Chief" to their resumes!

Create a Comic Strip (pg. 41)

Students create a comic strip based on their novel. They must then explain the central idea and mood of the strip.

Refer to your Sunday newspaper to show your students a quality sample.

Book Opinionnaire (pg. 42)

Do you agree or disagree with that statement?

Students create ten statements based on themes and ideas in their novel. They trade papers with another student who decides how he/she feels about the statements. Once the opinionnaire is returned to its owner, that student writes a one-page analysis that determines if his/her peer who filled out the opinionnaire would like or dislike the book. This assignment is all about analysis.

Analyze, analyze, analyze!

Disney Movie Project

In order to complete this assignment, you will need to watch **one** animated Disney movie. Movie options will be determined by your teacher. After selecting your movie, complete these worksheets while you view the film. If you do not have the movie you wish to use, ask your parent or guardian for assistance in obtaining it.

1. Design a front cover and attach it to these pages. Include artwork and the name of the movie. Also, include your name, the assignment title, your class period, and the date.

2. Label the plot diagram below by placing the following terms in order: resolution, rising action, initiating conflict, falling action, exposition, climax

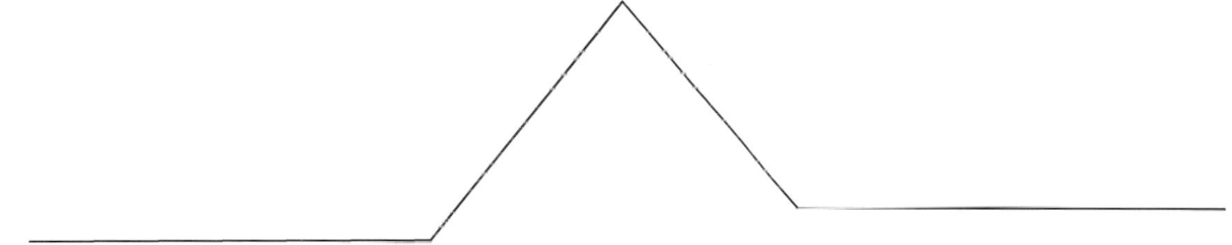

3. In the boxes below, <u>label and explain</u> each part of the movie's plot (the first box is labeled for you).

Exposition		

<u>Directions</u>: Write the definition of each *italicized* word and then answer the questions that follow.

Answer all questions in complete sentences (this does not apply to definitions).

4. *Protagonist-*____

Who is the protagonist?____

Do you like this character? Why or why not?_______________________________________

____

5. *Antagonist-*____

Who is the antagonist?____

Do you like this character? Why or why not?_______________________________________

____

6. *Conflict-*____

Explain the conflict between the protagonist and the antagonist.__________________________

____

____

____

7. *Foreshadowing-*____

Is there foreshadowing in this movie?   Yes   No

If so, explain. If not, provide your own example.____________________________________

____

____

____

8. *Flashback-*____

Is there a flashback in this movie? Yes No

If so, explain. If not, provide your own example.____________________________

____

____

____

9. *Personification-*____

Is there personification in this movie? Yes No

If so, explain. If not, provide your own example.____________________________

____

____

____

10. *Mood-*____

Describe a scene from this movie and explain the mood.________________________

____

____

____

11. *Theme-*____

Explain a theme found in this movie.____________________________________

____

____

____

12. *Characterization-*____

Describe a scene in which a character's personality is revealed.____________________

____

____

____

13. *Simile-*____

Is there a simile in this movie? Yes No

If so, write and explain the simile. If not, provide your own example.____________________

____

____

____

14. *Metaphor-*____

Is there a metaphor in this movie? Yes No

If so, write and explain the metaphor. If not, provide your own example.____________________

____

____

____

15. *Symbolism-*____

In the spaces below, draw symbols that represent the protagonist and the antagonist.

protagonist	antagonist

Name:_________________________________ Period:____________

Directions: In Box 1, write a narrative about yourself and a personal experience. In Box 2, use the story from Box 1 to write a biography about yourself and the experience. In Box 3, turn the story from Box 1 into a poem.

Box 1-Narrative

Box 2-Biography

Box 3-Poetry

Name:______________________________ Period:____________

Directions: Using the information from Boxes 1, 2, and 3, complete the following questions.

1. Compare and contrast Boxes 1 and 2.

____
____
____
____
____

2. Compare and contrast Boxes 2 and 3.

____
____
____
____
____

3. Compare and contrast Boxes 1 and 3.

____
____
____
____
____

4. Identify and explain an appropriate audience for each box.

____
____
____
____
____

5. Explain which form of writing was easiest for you to compose.

____
____
____
____
____

Use that Form: Fact, Fiction, and Fantasy

Name:________________________________ Period:____________

Directions: For this assignment, you will need a newspaper article from the news section of a local or national newspaper. Summarize this article in Box 1. Include critical details such as names, places, dates, and any other relevant facts. In Box 2, use the information from Box 1 to transform the text from fact to fiction or fantasy.

Box 1-Summary of News Article

Box 2-Fiction or Fantasy

Use that Form: Fact, Fiction, and Fantasy

Name:________________________________ Period:____________

Directions: Using the information from Boxes 1 and 2, complete the following questions.

1. Determine the central idea of Box 1.

____
____
____
____
____

2. Compare and contrast Boxes 1 and 2.

____
____
____
____
____

3. Identify and explain an appropriate audience for each box.

____
____
____
____
____

4. Explain how authors of fictional stories use or alter history to create their works.

____
____
____
____
____

5. Decide if it is easier to write a story based on fact, fiction, or fantasy. Explain your answer.

____
____
____
____
____

Flip & Roll

Name:________________________________ Period:____________

Directions:

1. Flip a coin.

    If the coin lands on heads, then write a fictional narrative.

    If the coin lands on tails, then write a science fiction narrative.

2. Roll a die twice.

The numbers you roll will determine which two literary terms must appear in your narrative.

    1-simile, 2-metaphor, 3-personification, 4-alliteration, 5-onomatopoeia, 6-allusion

3. Write your narrative below.

Coloring Conflict 1

Name:________________________________ Period:____________

Directions:
Color squares **green** if the conflict is *character vs. self.*
Color squares **orange** if the conflict is *character vs. nature*.
Color squares **purple** if the conflict is *character vs. society*.

If Sarah fails her test, her parents will ground her all weekend. Irene, the smartest student in class, sits next to Sarah on the day of the test. Sarah contemplates looking off of Irene's paper.

Joe is a smoker and believes he should be able to smoke anywhere he wants. The law says otherwise.

Tom saw his friend, Billy, steal some candy. Tom is very fond of Mr. Kelly, the storeowner.

Laura cries herself to sleep every time it storms.

Kevin ran as fast as he could because the tornado was gaining ground on him.

Mrs. Lampley joined the Red Cross so that she could help storm victims.

After a long day of working, Rosa Parks refused to give up her seat on the bus.

Jana is glad to be home from school. She hates going to school every day. In fact, she hates just about everything. When she is at school, she never works with other students because she thinks they will call her ideas stupid. When she gets home, all she does is read so that she doesn't have to think about her own life.

Mrs. Arnold, Katie's mom, is like a mom to Jessica. Jessica just saw Katie help herself to Mrs. Arnold's money.

Becky told a lie about her best friend, Dana. Now, Dana refuses to speak to Becky. Becky hates the fact that she lies, but she can't stop herself.

The 7th graders at Madison Middle School started a petition to end the school uniform policy.

Ben hates how everyone always wears expensive clothing brands. He wears a $5 t-shirt and $10 jeans every day because he wants to be unique.

Many people in Louisiana had to sleep in the Superdome after Hurricane Katrina destroyed their homes.

Tina knows that her friend, Rachel, likes Tony. The problem is that Tina also likes him. Tony asked Tina on a date.

The Smith family had to relocate after the earthquake destroyed their entire neighborhood.

Jake was texting while driving and hit a car. That car's driver died at the scene. Jake will never forgive himself.

Jennifer hates Santa Claus after receiving a lump of coal last year. She has started writing malls across the country to stop inviting Santa during December.

Coloring Conflict 2

Name:__________________________________ Period:____________

Directions: In each circle, create a short story containing conflict. Each type of conflict must be used three times. They should be scattered and not in any type of order. Trade papers with a partner who will color your circles based on the type of conflict presented.

Colors:
Color circles **red** if the conflict is *character vs. self.*
Color circles **yellow** if the conflict is *character vs. nature.*
Color circles **blue** if the conflict is *character vs. society.*

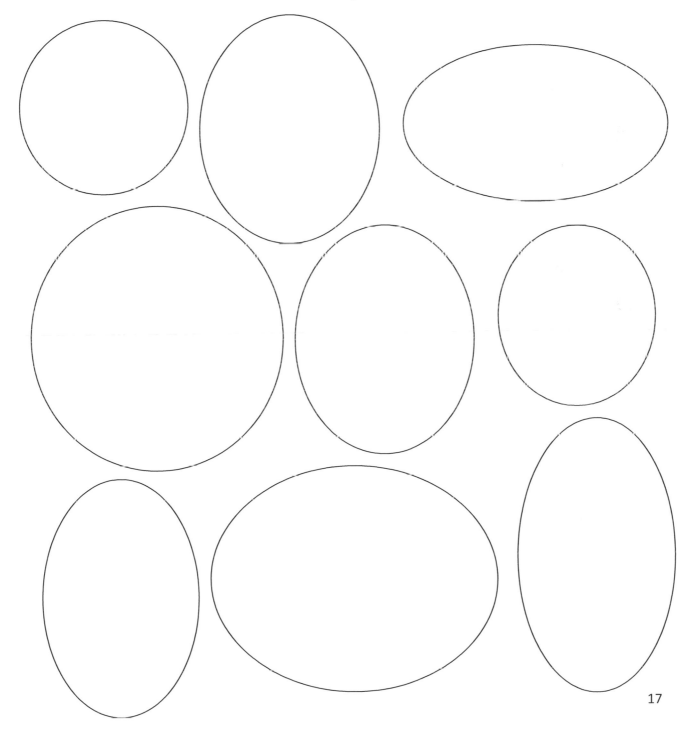

Flip It: Fact and Opinion

Name:_________________________________ Period:____________

Directions: Flip a coin 10 times. Record each flip on the chart below. "H" is for heads and "T" is for tails. For every heads you flip, write a sentence containing a fact. For every tails you flip, write a sentence containing an opinion. After all of your sentences are completed, trade papers with a partner. **Fold the paper so your partner cannot see where you recorded your flips.** In the last column, your partner will write "F" if the sentence is a fact and "O" if the sentence is an opinion. An example has been completed for you.

H or T:	Sentence:	F or O:
H	Northmont Middle School begins its school day at 7:45 a.m.	F

Fold Here

Flip It: Simile and Metaphor

Name:__________________________________ Period:_____________

Directions: Flip a coin 10 times. Record each flip on the chart below. "H" is for heads and "T" is for tails. For every heads you flip, write a sentence containing a simile. For every tails you flip, write a sentence containing a metaphor. After all of your sentences are completed, trade papers with a partner. **Fold the paper so your partner cannot see where you recorded your flips.** In the last column, your partner will write "S" if the sentence is a simile and "M" if the sentence is a metaphor. An example has been completed for you.

H or T:	Sentence:	S or M:
T	Drew was a glove, catching every baseball that came his way.	M

Fold Here

Flip It: Alliteration and Onomatopoeia

Name:________________________________ Period:____________

Directions: Flip a coin 10 times. Record each flip on the chart below. "H" is for heads and "T" is for tails. For every heads you flip, write a sentence containing alliteration. For every tails you flip, write a sentence containing onomatopoeia. After all of your sentences are completed, trade papers with a partner. **Fold the paper so your partner cannot see where you recorded your flips.** In the last column, your partner will write "A" if the sentence has alliteration and "O" if the sentence has onomatopoeia. An example has been completed for you.

H or T:	Sentence:	A or O:
H	Ben biked before breakfast.	A

Fold Here

Name that Symbol

Name:__________________________________ Period:_____________

Directions: Read all stories below and draw a related symbol for each. Explain your reasoning. Afterwards, create five stories on the back of this paper. A partner will draw and explain symbols for the stories that you created.

1. Jason loves the blue hat that his father gave him. His father had it specially made for Jason and it even had a yellow "J" embroidered on the front. The reason that this hat is so important to Jason is because it is the last present his father ever gave him. Sadly, Jason's father passed away last year.

2. Lily and Rose were best friends. They did absolutely everything together. They even dressed the same. One day, Lily and Rose got into a huge fight because Rose went to the eye doctor who informed her that she would have to wear glasses. Rose tried to explain things to Lily, but Lily wouldn't hear of it. Now that they wouldn't look the same, the friendship was over.

3. Things certainly changed the day that Garrett bought the winning lottery ticket. He bought a new house, a new car, and went on a lengthy vacation. Garrett even bought all of his friends and family members the presents that they wanted.

4. Brooke was home visiting from college. She enjoyed coming home because it was a nice break from dorm life. She loved sitting on her bed and looking through old pictures from when she was a little girl. She also loved seeing Mr. Snuggles, her beloved teddy bear.

5. Justin is as fast as a cheetah! He has enjoyed running ever since he was a little boy. He joined the track team in middle school and also ran track in high school and college. His goal is to participate in the Olympics.

Character
Name: ____________________

Your
Name: ____________________

Totem Pole Symbolism

Directions:

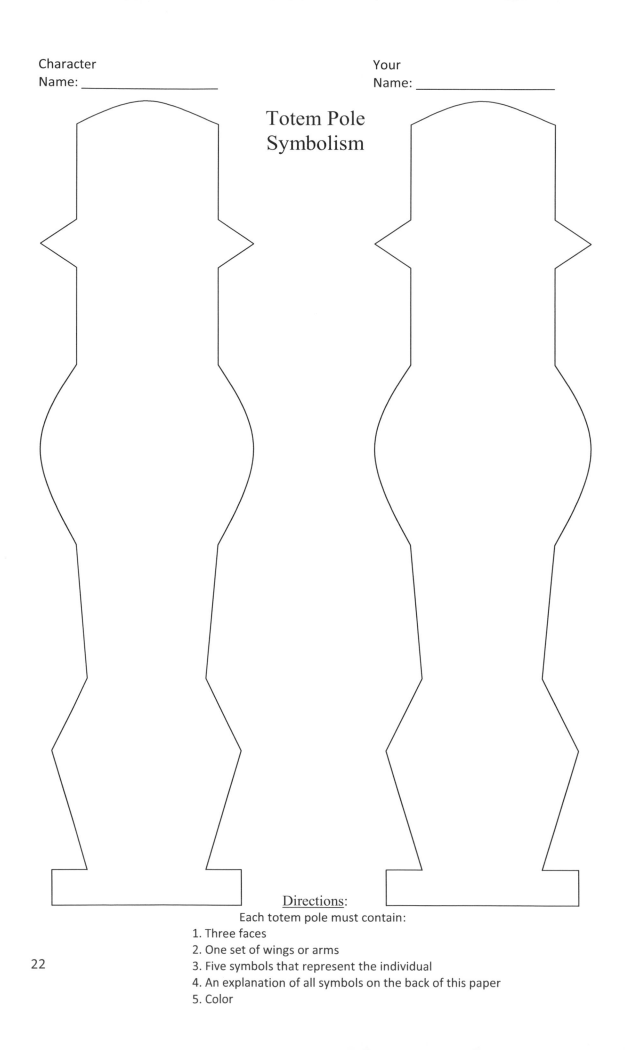

Each totem pole must contain:

1. Three faces
2. One set of wings or arms
3. Five symbols that represent the individual
4. An explanation of all symbols on the back of this paper
5. Color

Name:________________________________ Period:____________

Directions: In each box, draw and color a food item that is representative of a character from the text. For example, a food item that is made with many different ingredients might be compared to a complex character. Next to each box, explain why you linked each character with that particular food item.

Character: ________________________

Explanation:____________________________

Character: ________________________

Explanation:____________________________

Character: ________________________

Explanation:____________________________

Pass the Plot

Groups of six will collaborate to create a cohesive story by writing two sentences per plot point.

<u>Estimated time</u>: 20-25 minutes

<u>Materials</u>: labeled index cards, pencil, paper

<u>Procedures</u>:

1. Students will break into groups of six.
2. Each group member will receive an index card labeled with a different point from the plot diagram. The plot diagram points are exposition, initiating conflict, rising action, climax, falling action, and resolution.
3. Students will work collaboratively to create a story. While all students will contribute ideas for each plot point, the student with the labeled index card will ultimately determine the two sentences for that part of the plot.
4. <u>The finished product of each group is a 12-sentence story that makes sense and incorporates all plot points.</u>
5. Groups will present their stories to the class.

Plot Plate

<u>Directions</u>: Divide a paper plate into six even sections. Label each section with the following terms: exposition, initiating conflict, rising action, climax, falling action, and resolution. Under each label, draw a picture of an event from the text that occurs during that part of the plot. Under each picture, write a two-sentence summary describing what happened in that part of the plot. An example of what your paper plate should look like is shown below.

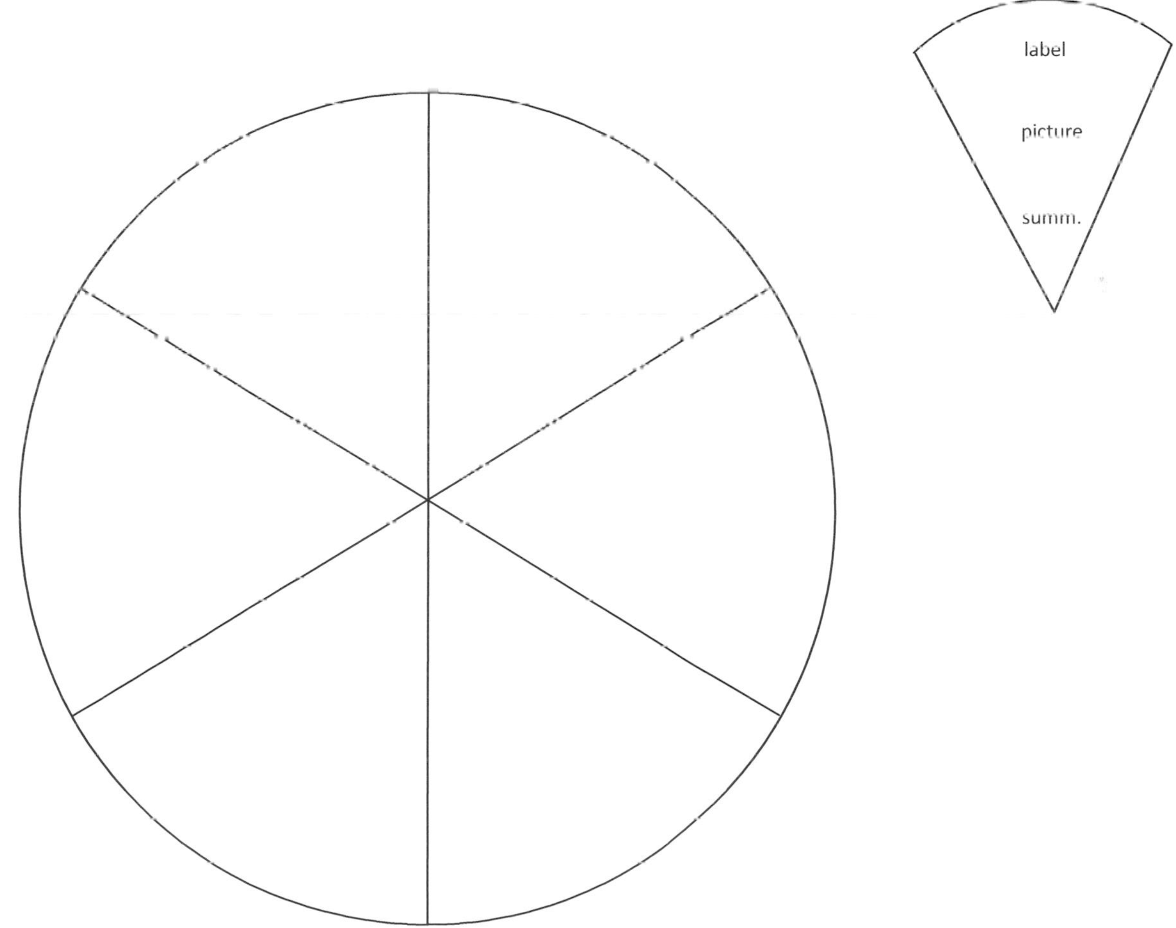

PLOT THAT SHOW

Name:_______________________________ Period:____________

You will be plotting the events of a television show. Complete this worksheet while you are watching the show. Ask your parent or guardian to determine an appropriate show for you to watch.

1. Label the plot diagram below by placing the following terms in order: resolution, rising action, initiating conflict, falling action, exposition, climax

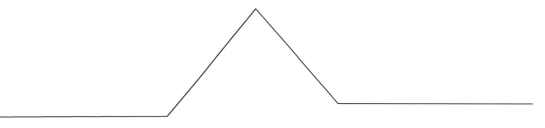

2. In the boxes below, label and explain each part of the show's plot (the first box is labeled for you).

Exposition		

3. Which part of the show's plot took the most amount of time? ______________________________

4. Which part of the show's plot took the least amount of time? ______________________________

5. Which part of the show's plot did you most enjoy? Why? ______________________________

____

Prewriting Worksheet

Name:________________________________ Period:____________

Directions: Complete the steps below and then create your story on a separate sheet of paper.

1. Setting: Roll a die and the number of your roll will determine the setting of your story.

1-__________________ 2-__________________ 3-__________________

4-__________________ 5-__________________ 6-__________________

2. Character development: Complete the boxes below to develop characters for your story.

Character name:	Physical description:
Interesting characteristic:	Other information:

3. Prewriting activity: Plot basic story events on the diagram below.

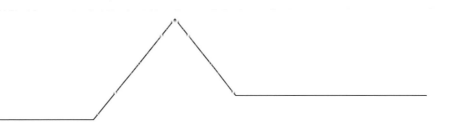

4. Figurative language: Your story must contain an example of personification, simile, and metaphor.

5. Descriptive details: Your story must explain what the characters see, hear, smell, touch, and taste.

Story title:	Mood:

Magazine Writing Activity

To begin this activity, cut out the following pictures from a magazine:

2-4 people

2 places (buildings, homes, landscapes, etc.)

3 miscellaneous objects (products from advertisements, etc.)

Directions: Create a one-page story based on the pictures that you cut out from your magazine. Use the guidelines below to provide some direction for your story.

People
The 2-4 people will be characters in your story. At least one character will be the protagonist and at least one character will be the antagonist.

Places
One place will be the setting at the beginning of your story. The other place will be the setting at the end of your story.

Miscellaneous Objects
One miscellaneous object will be a symbol for the protagonist's personality. For example, if you find an advertisement for a pack of Band-Aids in your magazine, this can represent how the protagonist helps situations to improve.

Another miscellaneous object will be a symbol for the antagonist's personality. For example, if you find a poison symbol in your magazine, this can represent how the antagonist makes others feel bad.

The last miscellaneous object will play an important role in your story. For example, if you find an advertisement for Nike shoes, these shoes must be important to your story. Perhaps your story is about running a race and the protagonist counts on his lucky Nike shoes to win, but the antagonist steals his shoes. The Nike shoes would then become an important part of the story.

Conflict
Your story will revolve around a character vs. character conflict. In other words, the characters are at odds with each other.

Writing your story

1. Introduce the characters and provide some background information about them. Explain the symbols for the characters as this will provide information about who they are or what they do.
2. Identify the initial setting and explain how it plays a role in your story.
3. Explain the conflict of your story and how the last miscellaneous object plays an important role.
4. Explain how the conflict is ultimately resolved.
5. Identify the final setting and explain how the character(s) arrived in this place.

Pasting your clippings

1. Paste your magazine clippings on a sheet of construction paper placed horizontally on your desk. Paste the protagonist on the far left side at the top, and the antagonist on the far left side at the bottom. Next to each character, paste the symbol that represents their personality.
2. To the right of the characters, paste the picture of the initial setting.
3. To the right of that, paste the object that plays an important role in your story.
4. On the far right side, paste the final setting.
5. Label all clippings on your construction paper.

Name:________________________________ Period:____________

Directions: For each scenario, explain what is being inferred and how you came to your conclusion. On a separate sheet of paper, create 10 scenarios of your own and a partner will determine what is being inferred.

1 Chris, a defense lawyer, bought a brand new $40,000 BMW. He was able to pay cash after saving for only a month.

2. Nate had to share a bedroom with his three brothers.

3. Mr. Carter owns many Michael Jackson CDs.

4. The Greene family had an expensive fence built around their enormous pool.

5. Sharon came home and discovered muddy footprints all over her white carpet. She followed the footprints upstairs and they stopped at her son's bedroom door.

Infer It

6. Blaze, the family dog, brought a Frisbee to his owner. The owner then put on his shoes and took the dog to the park.

7. Deena wanted to go to the mall to buy a new dress. She picked up the phone and called her best friend, Robin.

8. Brittany's neighbor, DeShaun, moved his Corvette out of the garage into the driveway. With his hose, he began filling a bucket with water.

9. Austin closed the door to his apartment and began walking to the store. After two minutes, he returned and grabbed his umbrella.

10. Kyle's family plans to stay in a Holiday Inn while on vacation. As Kyle was packing, he ran downstairs to ask his mom a question. As soon as he returned to his room, he put swim trunks in his suitcase.

ENHANCE YOUR VOCABULARY

Name:__________________________________ Period:_____________

Directions: Surround each of the words below with several alternative words.

a lot	cool	stuff
things	like	said
paper	go	tell
make	good	big
small	old	nice
whole	done	look

Nutrition Facts and Ingredients

Name:____________________________________ Period:______________

<u>Directions</u>**:** For this activity, you will need two nutrition facts labels with their ingredients. The labels should be for similar, but not identical food items (i.e., different flavors or brands). Paste your label and ingredient information for both food items in the spaces below.

Item 1:________________________________
Nutrition Facts and Ingredients

Item 2:________________________________
Nutrition Facts and Ingredients

On a separate sheet of paper, use the nutrition facts and ingredients to answer the following questions in complete sentences:

1. Which product has more calories?
2. Which product has a lesser total carb. count?
3. How many ingredients are in Product 1? Product 2?
4. Compare and contrast the two products. Be sure to include information from the nutrition facts as well as the ingredients.
5. Based on all of the information, which product do you consider to be healthier? Support your answer with evidence from the labels and ingredients.

Coupons

Name:________________________________ Period:__________

Directions: For this activity, you will need two coupons. The coupons should be for similar, but not identical items (i.e., different brands). Paste your coupons in the spaces below.

Item 1:______________________________ **Coupon**	**Item 2:**______________________________ **Coupon**

On a separate sheet of paper, use the coupons to answer the following questions in complete sentences:

1. Which coupon has the closest expiration date?
2. Identify the restrictions of your coupon.
3. Are your coupons able to be used at all locations?
4. Compare and contrast the coupons. Refer to information from numbers 1, 2, and 3.
5. Based on all of the information, which coupon do you believe is the better bargain?

Name:______________________________ Period:___________

Directions: Create an instant message conversation between ________________ and ________________ based on pages _____-_____ from the text. Use different colors to fill in the boxes below, and then write a character's name on the line next to each box. Write each character's dialogue using the color from your key. Include the character's name to the left of the dialogue, so it is clear who typed what.

Key:

☐ ____________

☐ ____________

Character:	Dialogue:

Hit the Cell

Name:_________________________________ Period:______________

Directions: Create a phone conversation between ____________________ and ____________________ based on pages ______ - ______ from the text. Use different colors to fill in the cell phones below, and then write a character's name on the line next to each phone. In the "Who's Speaking?" column, color all of the phones according to your key, so it is clear who is talking on each line.

Key: ____________________ ____________________

Who's Speaking?

slide to unlock

Name:______________________________ Period:____________

Book:_________________________

Chapter:
Summary:

Critical detail:

Prediction:

Question you would ask ____________:

Chapter:
Summary:

Critical detail:

Prediction:

Question you would ask ____________:

Chapter:
Summary:

Critical detail:

Prediction:

Question you would ask ____________:

Create a Soundtrack

Name:_______________________________ Period:____________

Imagine your novel is being turned into a movie and five scenes from the book must be accompanied by music.

Directions: Design a cover for your soundtrack. Your cover design must include the title and author of the book. Complete the chart below. On the back of this paper, identify all five scenes from the book and explain your song selections (3-5 sentences per scene/song).

	SONG	ARTIST(S)	PG#
1.			
2.			
3.			
4.			
5.			

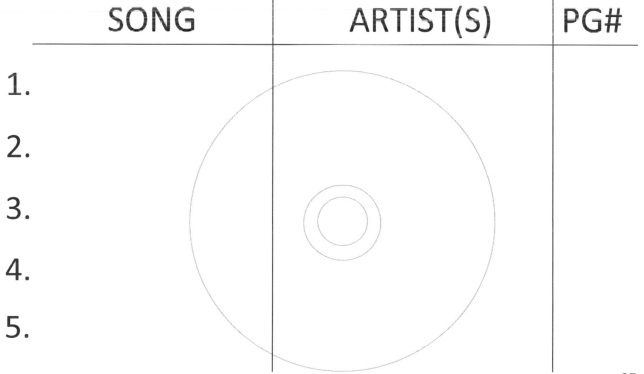

Bime line (a book time line)

Name:_______________________________ Period:____________

Directions: Choose six pages from the text and use the boxes below to summarize those pages. This must be done in chronological order and each box must contain three sentences. On the back of this paper, create a colored illustration of your favorite scene.

Page:

Page:

Page:

Page:

Page:

Page:

Book Brochure

Directions:

- For this brochure, you need a blank sheet of computer paper folded into three equal sections, like an informational pamphlet.
- Select three chapters from your novel and complete the following:
  - Create a one-paragraph summary (5-7 sentences) for each chapter
  - Draw a symbol or identify a literary term for each chapter
  - Identify and define five vocabulary words
  - Create three higher-level thinking questions
  - Identify two self-to-text connections (ex: Ryan moved from TN to FL and I moved from GA to OH)
  - Develop two questions you would ask the author about the book
- On the cover:
  - Write the title of the novel
  - Draw and color a picture representative of the text
  - Include your name in the bottom right corner

To assist you with creating your brochure, a layout is illustrated below. After folding your brochure, begin labeling Side One headings that are underlined. Information should be copied in the same order as you see here. After Side One is finished, begin Side Two. Make sure that the summary for your first chapter is on the back of the front cover. Make sure your writing is not upside down.

Side One

<u>Five defined vocabulary terms</u> __________ <u>Three higher-level thinking questions</u>	<u>Two self-to-text connections</u> __________ <u>Two questions for the author</u>	(cover) <u>Title</u> (picture) (name)

Side Two

<u>Summary for</u> (insert chapter #) __________ <u>symbol</u> or <u>literary term</u>	**<u>Summary for</u>** (insert chapter #) __________ <u>symbol</u> or <u>literary term</u>	**<u>Summary for</u>** (insert chapter #) __________ <u>symbol</u> or <u>literary term</u>

Editor-in-Chief

Create a magazine cover, along with three articles, on the following topic:

____

Your magazine cover must:

- State the name of the magazine (relevant to your event/topic)
- State your name in the bottom right corner
- State three subheadings of articles that appear in your magazine
- State the issue month and year (time period should be relevant to your event/topic)
- List a realistic price that the magazine would sell for in that time period
- Be neat, creative, and colorful

Your three articles must:

- Be on three separate pages (stapled to the cover)
- Have headings (identical to the subheadings on the cover)
- Summarize, in your own words, the event/topic you are researching
- Cite at least one source (website, textbook, etc.)

Below is a layout to assist you with completing this project:

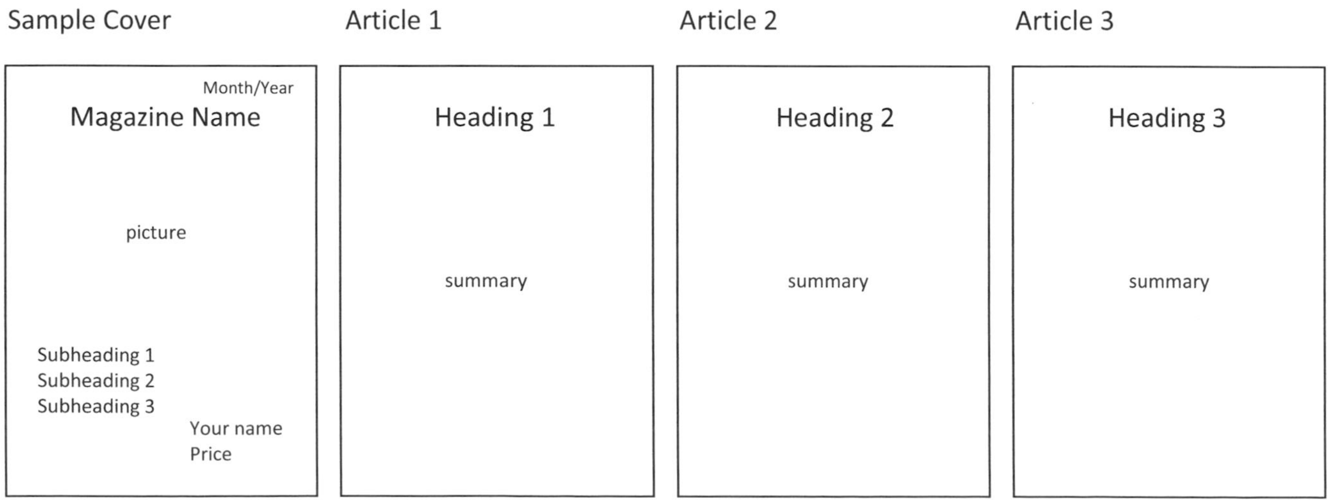

Sample Cover	Article 1	Article 2	Article 3
Month/Year Magazine Name picture Subheading 1 Subheading 2 Subheading 3 Your name Price	Heading 1 summary	Heading 2 summary	Heading 3 summary

Create a Comic Strip

Name:________________________________ Period:____________

Directions: Fill in the boxes with characters, captions, events, and settings from the text. Separate scenes using vertical lines and color when finished. Explain the central idea and mood that appear in your comic strip.

Central idea:	Mood:

Book Opinionnaire

Name:______________________________ Period:___________

Directions: Create a 10-statement opinionnaire based on themes and ideas mentioned in your book. Look especially for themes and ideas that appear throughout your novel. For example, if a character in your novel repeatedly lies, but feels it is justified, a statement on your opinionnaire could be:

1. Lying is acceptable in certain situations.
Strongly Agree (SA) Agree (A) Disagree (D) Strongly Disagree (SD)

Record your 10 statements below. Once you are finished, trade papers with a peer who has not read your book and your peer will circle his or her answers. *Analyze the results, and then write a one-page paper explaining why you believe your peer would like or dislike the book. IN YOUR ANALYSIS, YOU MUST CITE EVIDENCE FROM HOW YOUR PEER ANSWERED YOUR OPINIONNAIRE TO RECEIVE FULL CREDIT.*

1.____
______________________________________ SA A D SD

2.____
______________________________________ SA A D SD

3.____
______________________________________ SA A D SD

4.____
______________________________________ SA A D SD

5.____
______________________________________ SA A D SD

6.____
______________________________________ SA A D SD

7.____
______________________________________ SA A D SD

8.____
______________________________________ SA A D SD

9.____
______________________________________ SA A D SD

10.____
______________________________________ SA A D SD

Made in the USA
San Bernardino, CA
23 February 2014